"In this collection, the anecdotal melds with the experiential...We encounter verses that serve as a template for the lyrical, the deployment of narratives and folksy idioms that are enchanting. [The] journey motif flutters from Nigeria to Canada, as the author attempts to bridge borders...Otiono offers us a poetic sacrament."

— **The Sunday Sun**

"Nduka Otiono is a poet of the musical word... His erudition blends seamlessly with the spoken sacred word of the local lore in poetry that is at once memorable and sophisticated. He wrenches love from the Nigerian nightmare with an uncommon touch at the instance and distance of an alien shore. He breaks bold ground in borderless intercourse, a noble feat that conjures up the landscape and dreamscape of Joseph Brodsky and Pablo Neruda."

— **Uzor Maxim Uzoatu**, award-winning author of *God of Poetry*

"Here are poems to enter into and live in and live by. The personal, the communal, the planetary inhabit these cosmic collages that stylistically stride from oral structures to the architectonics of the written. Nduka Otiono's poetic stance is that of defiant disruption and truth-telling. Read this book and feel the pulse."

— **Uche Nduka**, *award-winning author of fourteen volumes of poetry*

LOVE IN A TIME OF NIGHTMARES

Nduka Otiono

Kika,

This is for you,
April child shadowed with dreams
and dancing to the footfalls of stubborn rain.

Contents

Acknowledgments

"Where the spirit does not work with the hand there is no art."
— Leonardo da Vinci

This collection has benefitted from the criticism of members of the Friday Group, Department of English and Film Studies, University of Alberta, Edmonton, Canada—especially Bert Almon, witty poet, professor, and coordinator. The Friday meetings provided the primary audience to test these poems and to receive valuable feedback. It also offered an excellent turf for cross-pollination of my essentially African, and my colleagues' Canadian poetics. For this I am most indebted to them, and to celebrated poet, Fred Wah, who shared his experience and craft with us one Friday in November 2006. The journey to Edmonton where most of these poems were written may not have been possible without the FS Chia Fellowship awarded to me by the University of Alberta. For this, I am most grateful. So am I, too, to The William Joiner Centre for War and Social Consequences, University of Massachusetts, Boston, for a Spring 2007 fellowship that enabled me to complete work on this volume.

I am beholden to Onookome Okome, Paul Ugor, Osonye Tess Onwueme, Pius Adesanmi, Dic Willie, Calixthus Okorowa, Gabriel Olayinka, Marco Katz, Idowu Ohioze, Emem and Kelechi Madu, and Norah Bowman, for their support.

There are others, friends, colleagues, and staff of the Department of English and Film Studies, University of Alberta, who though less visible, have contributed to the production of this book. I thank them all.

For opportunities to initially publicly share earlier versions of a few of these poems, I am grateful to David Martin and the Olive Reading Series Group of Edmonton; Askold Melnyczuk and the Arrowsmith group for a reading at Lame Duck Books, Harvard Square, Cambridge Massachusetts; *Sentinel Poetry Magazine* (online), and *Stimulus Magazine*.

My profound appreciation extends to the wide community of poets from whom I have imbibed the fluid ecstasy of honeyed words. For copyright permissions, I am particularly grateful to Patrick Friesen, Tanure Ojaide, Obiageli Okigbo, Kevin Bowen, Nguyen Duy and Nguyen Ba Chung, and to Christy and Karl Siegler for "Interface" from *Dwell* by Jeff Derksen, copyright 1994, Talon Books Ltd., Vancouver. (Reprinted in The New Long Poem Anthology, ed. Sharon Thesen copyright 2001, Talon Books Ltd., Vancouver.)

Finally, devoid of the patience and support of my family who understood the need for this intellectual pilgrimage, the muse may still have been in flight. Now, how do I convey a lifetime appreciation for their endurance of my nomadic absences?

Author's note for the second edition

For this second edition of the book, published on the 15th anniversary of its original publication, the publisher and I have taken the liberty to make some editorial and design changes. These include a new cover and light editing of the poems to address errors in the first issue. I acknowledge my publishing consultant, Kolade Olanrewaju Freedom, for his professionalism in the project. I am grateful to Richard Mammah, journalist, reading culture promoter, and proprietor of Mace Associates Ltd, for his abiding confidence in my work.

Ottawa, December 2023

And what errand can I run
for the spider whose web
has become refuge for my desires?
ageless diviner, sage
of all seasons,
I have brought offerings
to the crossroads
where I need the right turn.
— Tanure Ojaide, "Reclamation"

We can see a day when borders will mean nothing
more than knowing where to cut your lawn.
— Jeff Derksen, "Interface."

PART ONE:
Rivers Within

Rivers Within
(Call and Response)

I have traced many rivers of love within.
My heart is full of love songs pleading...

There are veins flowing with sad songs.
Daily I think of uncharted landscapes within.

Some arteries ferry bitter memories of love.
Like cancer, some loves never stop spreading.

I have fetched laughters from Obida's[*] depths.
The waves ripple gently like nipples pleading.

The banks of my heart are a bed for ecstasy.
My request is like a blank cheque pending.

Like Langston Hughes, I've known rivers ancient...
You are the mermaid, heroine of my rivers within.

---

[*] Obida — a stream in the poet's homeland revered for its mystical powers.

You've stained my verses with stanzas of heartbreak
Passion is the fish swimming in rivers receding.

How do you fish in shallow waters full of effluents?
Dead water hyacinths floating on oil need weeding.

You are the deep river goddess I'm still navigating.
Your naked eye cannot see the signals I'm sending.

Gauge the blood pressure in the bivalves of my heart.
Can a love surgeon dam the surging waters within?

Did I hear you say, Obida does not eat stones, Nduka?
I'm now a fugitive lover with a heart that's bleeding.

Rooms We Live In

We walk from streetlight to streetlight
silence to silence
how to speak about human heart and memory
how to speak about all the rooms we live in
—Patrick Friesen, "Anna"

As from silhouette to nightmare, so from
Birth to death we live from room to room.
Conceived in a room inside woman,
We swim in forever-warm amniotic waters
Until nature evicts us, debtors with unpaid
Boarding and lodging bills out of sight.
So, what is man that I am mindful of him?
Forever a child searching for teats, from
Mother to wife, like a butterfly in flight,
We walk from streetlight to streetlight.

How do I begin to sing about mother?
Tireless creditor to errant children,
Always welcoming all to her room.
Only yesterday, I saw her in a dream,
Rosary in one hand, in the other olive oil
To anoint a son continually travelling in silence
When the road is spread-eagled, impatient

Like grandma's pipe yearning for tobacco—
Inside her room, smoke and ashes become incense,
And the air is still, blowing from silence to silence.

Some rooms come as rites of passage—Classrooms,
Offices, bars or one I was given at adolescence,
Where I learnt to sing songs of experience,
The fire of pubescence burning in my loins.
Each day was riddled with escapades as I
Returned from one friend's room with one story
Or another, after sharing unspent cigarette stubs
And remnants in elders' palmwine kegs—
How do I remember all the rooms with history?
How to speak about human heart and memory?

How do I speak about that eternal, lonely room
Into which I'll retire, unaware of its location or for
How long I'll live there before the last Judgement.
How do I know what happens amongst the dead?
"Death makes us all look ridiculous," a poet said.
Between casket and grave which is the last room?
There, we'll return, sand house and bones, uninvited
Tenants with unpaid boarding and lodging bills.
Between womb and tomb where's peace within?
How else to speak about all the rooms we live in?

Grandma's Pipe

She's been long dead
But she returns with
Every pipe I see,
Old woman with the pipe,
Chip of the rare breed.

She would sit leisurely on her
Ancient bed in the family house,
A red mud platform that
To keep cool and soothing,
She would scrub daily with
Dead roots of plantain trees,
Fresh like wet bath sponge.

Then the ritual would begin—

First, she would sort the tobacco,
Rolls of golden brown leaves
So unique and so aromatic
You are tempted to sniff them.
Grandma would caress every part
Of it with the tenderness of
An experienced weaver in a loom.
Next, she would load her pipe,
Brown like the tobacco leaves,

Curved upwards as though
Swearing allegiance to her.
In turn, she would stroke it gently
Taking her time around the bend
Like a driver at a dangerous corner.
Then she would take a break
To fetch a piece of burnished coal
From the busy fireplace,
Admire the loaded pipe as if
Reluctant to hurt it with fire.
She would hesitantly drop the red
Coal onto the soul of the pipe,
Raise it to a crooked angle onto
Her mouth & so suck with the urgency
Of a baby breastfeeding hungrily
You would think she was about to choke.

Then she would relax, as if meditating
Or perhaps pondering a joke...

She would puff the smoke,
Spiral it upwards as if
Towards heavensgate,
A contented smile lighting up
Her dry, wrinkled face.

Again she would relax, as if meditating...

Then her head would jerk like one
Who's just regained consciousness.

"Nduka nwaam...Mhuum..."

A long pause tells a thousand and one tales.

So, one day I seize the cue and ask
When and how she picked up the habit.
"That's another story," she offers in native tongue:

"Once your father's father was sick during Biafra
And I was alone with him, the great Obosi,
Champion wrestler that never lost a fight.
His fiery eyes were enough to defeat his foes.
They shone like the sun at midday,
Rolling in their orbs...
Because the world revolved around them."

Another draught of smoke and sparks fly...

"Everyone else had run to the bush, Nduka *nwam*,
And I was alone with your father's father
And fever had so wracked his body
One could boil corn on it.

And he was once again a child.
Well, not as if men are not always chill…"

Her words trail off
As she casts her eyes on the wall,
Tracing the delicate Uli patterns on them…

When she stirs, her eyes are moist,
And sadness overshadows her face.

"See that hole on the wall there," she points,
"Look at the other one on the ceiling there:
That's where the bullet flew in,
Unexpected thunderbolt from the devil,
Bounced off the wall and hit Obosi,
Strongman with a soft heart,
Dispenser of gifts, scourge of wicked men
Who defeated Ono and restored justice,
Earning a moniker that became family name."

Silence upon silence upon silences…
But there's no science to salience—
A resilient spirit is a gift from God.
The eye never sheds blood no matter the sting.

She raises her charming pipe aloft…

"This was Obosi's pipe," she continues.

"Grief and loneliness are worse than death.

War is a ruthless demon that unleashes tragedies.

I am sole witness to the painful fall of a great man.

And I died that day, only this sand & ashes remain.

(She pulls the skin on her left arm violently)

Only this pipe remains—

My comforter, my memory, my courage, my gun.

No smoke issuing from it is ordinary, but an ordinance.

They are gun smoke from every shot I aim in vengeance.

And I'll continue to shoot his killers until death do us join.

Halloween Night
(Two voices, to an acoustic guitar)

Ghost-filled silence of a Halloween night,

inside my room, two clocks tick in conversation

like security guards with walkie-talkies,

watchmen for a lonesome poet.

> Outside, the oft-busy road is quiet tonight
>
> as earth is whitewashed with sandy snow
>
> stretching across fields with its cold glow.
>
> Still, its feathered flakes continue to fall
>
> as if to justify the season's name: fall.

Sometimes it reminds of the Fall of man—

how Adam proved his love for Eve

and ate of the forbidden fruit. Fall

brings desire to an intemperate lonely

heart craving for that warmth only

Love's fire and lyre can deliver.

> I've become a bachelor again,
>
> alien in a material world
>
> separated from family and friends
>
> by demands of the knowledge factory
>
> dispensing wisdom and cant
>
> to a poet with a documentary impulse.

It's Halloween night, alright,

and I'm learning new harmonies

of Edmonton's fecund culture, straining

to hear the music of her winds, tonight forgetting

to tender candies to strangers at the door—

children on a surreal seasonal ritual,

screeching like owls and mocking death.

       Tonight, the teevee shows *Inside Hell House*

       and a priest calls on every mortal to pray—

"Forgive us our trespasses, Lord,

as we forgive those who trespass against us,

and look not upon our hearts

but upon our humble faith."

       But how do I kneel to pray on a Halloween night

       when ghosts from another plane crash haunt me?*

---

*   Reference to the October 29, 2006 crash of the Abuja to Sokoto ADC Airlines Flight 053 (ADK053) in Nigeria. 96 of the 105 passengers on board perished.

Paint the Sky

it's a wet, breezy Friday night
and I will paint the sky tonight
inspired by my wrinkled jacket,

a raincoat that reminds me
of the gossamer feel of condoms.
I'm in an Edmonton bar, alone,

dreaming of homeland and Maxim
with all the Stars, pepper soup and
ugba salad that Friday night offers...

inside Ratt, there're no rats.
the bar is clean like a newly shaved chin
but instead of the fragrance of aftershave

the smell of tobacco hangs in the air
suffocating desire with nicotine
and I, a troubadour, am perched

on a stool with spindly legs like
the stilts of some African
masquerade, facing the window...

outside, Edmonton is the
tortured splash of
incandescent bulbs...

from my glassy hotspot I see
angels of darkness in flight
with no compass to locate my condo
shadowed somewhere in the horizon
where-in I've grown weary from
keeping vigils for a dreaded winter

as each day glides past with
expectations of nature's frozen temper.
tonight, I see red in the air for

"Red is freedom road," F.O* said
and red is Ratt's Star outlined
by colour blue that reminds

me of hurrying cumulus outside...
I will paint the sky red tonight
when the clouds are spread out

----

* Nigerian playwright, Femi Osofisan. One of his plays is entitled *Red is the Freedom Road.*

like the wings of an eagle in mid flight.
I see floating atop the watery film
of my favourite beverage, pictures of

Edmonton's rousing skyline
but cannot find buried somewhere
in her valley, her river of peace.

at the west end, clouds gather like wools
drifting towards this 'room at the top.'
inside the bar, Edmonton is a chatter of

tongues converging from distant
climes on this dragging Friday night–
but between Power Plant and Ratt

there are no signs of Joel with
Bagger, and his advance party,
poets on a mission to pour

libations to their Muse.
now in this suspended bar,
lonely, I wander through a maze

of temptations beckoning
like Irish cream and thinking
of special Thanksgiving turkeys

and the festivities in the air
for tonight I shall paint the sky
inspired by my wrinkled jacket,

a raincoat that reminds me of
the gossamer feel of condoms.
alone in this Edmonton bar

I dream of homeland and
all the guns and crude oil
in combat in the Niger delta.

A Memory of Berkeley
(For Robert Hass, Malcolm Margolin, and Toby Wolff)

Here
the world
meets you through poets in a
concert of words on a sidewalk.
the words summon you,
sacred unction in communion
with Mother earth.

Far from California's crazy infernos,
on this east shore of San Francisco Bay
a cornucopia of silk-screened words
 rise to meet you at Addison Street,
and poets, step by step, tease
time and space with porcelain
enamel texts on cast-iron plates.

Here, a gathering of poets
tile by tile mingle history and
emotions of a shared destiny.
wayfarer in search of lost words,
you have travelled from Boston
bursting with traffic on Friday nights
to trace this coalition of the willing—poets,
patrons, architects, technocrats
united in vision to worship Words.

Here's the hub of the world,
a short whisper away from
Free Speech Circle at UCB
where in some gorgeous library,
Mark Twain sits, daydreaming of
San Francisco's art-rage: from City Lights
to Addison Street before Silicon Valley
emerged from the menacing fog
to hoodwink a generation lost
on the information superhighway.

Still, on Berkeley's Poetry Walk
words are the world's emperor
and poets are her royal majesties
robed in such metaphoric fineries
you will quietly genuflect
to their verbal legacies.
From the Ohlone song,
"See! I am dancing!
On the rim of the world I am dancing,"
seraphic voices shepherd you through
this streetscape, some whispering like
Yosano Akiko, others howling like
Allen Ginsberg and his Beat Generation.
together they resurrect in plates that
patina into antique hue, igniting
nostalgia for Clark's Ibadan

and its running splash of rust and gold.

Here the world meets you
through poets in a concert
of words on a sidewalk; the
words become "One" in
John Roberts' emblematic
poem, invite you to
rediscover the aura
of an era.

It's Fall Again

It's fall again
and the leaves rain like confetti
spreading on the wedding floor of
A couple's heart in September
when Barry remembered
first time he met his love.

The winds usher them,
gold leaves shuffling
and rustling carefreely
outside St Anthony's on Wyte Ave.
where the couple's fantasies burst
with flashes from digital cameras

It's fall again
and their hearts are chapters of crises
I can read with my eyes shut -
I, amateur fortune-teller, read hearts
like a hunter of surprises beneath protective
casings of molluscs hidden under
Fall's leaves crackling and dancing
to windsongs like models on a catwalk.

It's fall again
And if you listen
you will hear the leaves conversing,
hear the jazz of their cackles
oblivious of the September wedding
and the coming Edmonton winter
with its wicked snow that harasses me.

It's fall again
and I'm thinking of 'ember months,
and their end-of-year rush.
I'm thinking of Christmas and the season's gifts:
coughs, thick coats and choruses.
I'm thinking of the couple
wearing their love like an uncomfortable necklace
outside St Anthony's Catholic church.

Love and Incense

At sunrise and at sundown
she fills her room with incense
chanting strange mantras
that lull him to dreamland.

her ritual is a spell
that en-trances a vagrant lover
and makes him her prisoner of love
wondering if tomorrow will ever come.

inside her dark sanctuary, objects of decor
are arranged like playmates on a chessboard
and her extra-white teeth sparkle
in invitation for another kiss.

He's been one week her guest,
fed on love and incense and lust
while each day tells a different story
of disconsolate fidelity in captivity.

Where is the covenant that binds the soul
when the spirit is locked in conflict
with the flesh? Where is the heart
that weds the head in times of sorrow?

There are hidden narratives in her eyes,
a hurtful past hangs with old pictures on her wall.
The fading tattoos on her feet and hands
express her desire for the memories to disappear.

But the memories remain, obstinate echoes
of a besotted hubby who'd host-aged her, until
like Saul, the scales fell from her eyes and she
escaped, seeking freedom in solitude and incense.

Thus every sunrise and every sundown,
she would fill her dim room with incense
and overwhelm her prisoner with scented love
offering herself like an angel from the shadows.

If only the night would swallow them,
lovebirds on a retreat forbidden;
If only the incense will anaesthetize them
Their wishes will hatch an incubating dream.

Lovesick

i'm still tracking the mythologies of love
as thoughts of u crystallize into a postcard
i'll keep in a locket mother gave me.

evening approaches and u bolt the gates
of ur heart, leaving me outside, struggling
to find new keys to unlock ur fading feelings.

night falls and loneliness invites, threatening
to seduce me with its delirious hymns and
leaves me scratching with desire for u.

it's mysterious how love's melodies change,
how its temper fluctuates like tidal waves—
flourishing at one moment then retreating.

i'll sit patiently here, waiting for the talcum
freshness of dawn to toast u again, for these
days u've become another familiar outsider.

morning comes and i'll knock on ur heart yet again,
after the nightmares of a lonely night i'll knock,
hoping u'll let me in to sing new lovesongs to u.

i'm lovesick, tired of the politics of our lives;
my love can be as stubborn as the moon,
now u see her now u don't and the cycle continues.

and when u let me in, i'll make u so high as my lover
u'll cherish me and be forever drunk with the hangover.

Chatting

love is never
enough across the miles.
a million smiles hide
behind the computer screen
as two poets chat
across seas and continents.
her voice is the tendril of spring:
"and time is going so fast
sometimes it's so boring
to spend all your time—
only working and burning
your emotions on
the cold fire of duty."

between the lines
there are discovery channels
to burning emotions
lost in a world where
words become needles
that arc-puncture dead souls,
and leave love never
enough across the miles.

Love in a Time of Nightmares

I no longer sleep, Shahrazad,
Since that encounter with you,
Spinner of yarns,
I no longer sleep...
Nights unroll with new tales,
And you stroll through the
Arteries of my heart.
You
      You
            You
Are the naked fires in my dream,
Burning coal in the harmattans of life
Burn, coal, burn...
Earth, wind and fire escort me
Fuelling the crackling embers
Of a dying regime
Whose generals die in jet crashes
And others metamorphose
Into latter-day demon-cats.

I walk with you, Shahrazad,
Through streets in spirit land
Thinking of Okigbo and Biafra's dead.
I walk through the ruins of dreamland

Thinking of demon-crazy politicians
Lost in a maze of old poli-tricks.

I no longer sleep, my love,
For there are no lamb tales
From parliament, only howls, hooting & looting

O Shahrazad,
You are the chloroform of my dreams,
I smell you in the seams of my pyjamas
Beyond the blood-letting in Persia,
I sleep-walk in bushes of terrorists,
And night filled with nightmares
Leaves my eyes burnishing like bonfires
Rekindling the suns of Independence.

Sharazad, my love,
Out of the depths you rise and smile
And I'm the gap between your teeth,
The empty spaces
That seek the dentist's attention.
I am your untutored suitor,
Lost in an age of oil wars
Unable to raise the bride price.

I am the jobless youth
Smoking cannabis in the alleys

And thinking of Canaan land.
I am your Sunday-Sunday Pastor,
Preacher-man with a passion for tithes

Light my candles, O Shahrazad,
Keep the spell blazing
For you are the theme of my dreams
And like California wildfires
I drift across passion land
Hoping to anchor in your bosom

But here I am, Shahrazad,
Where love abandoned me,
Here I am,
Prostrate like a tired phallus
After a long night.

Flesh and Spirit

he's gone the way of all flesh
plucking leaves of grace from
her forest of a thousand passions

love has blindfolded him
lost in a grove, struggling
to discover the channels within

last night he had the nightmares again
caught in the branchwork of spiders,
governors of his country, his lover

he's learning to speak in tongues to
cure her fiery songs of despair that singe
his flesh and sting his kissable lips—

then he'll go the way of spirits
chanting *aluta continua* all night

Archive Fever
(For Jeannine Green and David Gay)

Chaucer didn't look happy when we visited.
He sat on a horse hemmed in between
musty Ellesmere's covers, a tired pilgrim
who had lost his honour.
He didn't know where he was either—
inside the special collections section
of Rutherford library, calm as a cemetery.
But he kept sparkling company, fellow
talebearers from the United Kingdom,
all, part of a colonial bequest.
There was John Bunyan, lost in his pilgrim's progress.
Milton was there too, rediscovering his paradise lost.
Jane Austen glowed with feminist pride and prejudice,
not persuaded by Emma and concerns for memory and
time, nor by the temperaments of sense and sensibility.
She didn't seem to care about Cupid any more
and the nightmares that wrap love.
Oh, and there was William Wordsworth, romanticist
trying to recollect emotions in tranquillity.
"This is from Jonathan Wordsworth, the
literary executioner of Wordsworth's estate,"
says the librarian, passionate guardian of the archive.
Her eyes are like apertures to the writers' lives.
Forever smiling, she maps the treasured walls

between the pages like reels rolling.

Enter Shakespeare, so content with his stature

as a playwright he doesn't mind being called W.S.

So great he left poetry and name to honour Wordsworth.

King of the stage, he's magnificent in a fourth edition folio.

And the visitor's eyes widened with great expectations,

smothered by a smouldering reputation

shouldered by time, art and fame.

Finally, there was Charles Dickens, vagrant of the city,

Master of romantic side of familiar things, staggering

with nineteen pamphlets of David Copperfield,

but with our mutual friend, Oliver Twist, nowhere in sight.

"Dickens was so fussy about his illustrations," says

the librarian, as if in an old curiosity shop.

In two months it will be Christmas, but there

was no time to contemplate a Christmas carol

as we left our enchanting new buddy,

bodies tempered by a new archive fever.

And someone remained to converse with Chaucer,

to confirm whether his name really meant "shoemaker."

University of Work

He crouches like the hunchback
In Arabian Night's entertainment
Each time he hauls onto his rear,
His multicoloured rucksack
Filled with assignments
And heavy books
Full of arcane knowledge
And inanities of lonely authors.

Then he thinks of Rutherford
Lost in tomes stacked in bookcases
And remembers that wall gecko again
Hunting book worms
In the Presidential library at Aso Rock—
These are times he sings:
"I love my books I won't lie,
Inside them I'll live and die."

If he means it, I won't know,
But I'll never forget the times
He's whispered like a lunatic
Calling U of A University of Work
And blaming nature for his woes
Like the poet stuck in the attic

While hurricane Katrina
Swelled like ripe pus.

Back in his room on Monday nights,
He'll tarry in front of his broken mirror
Staring at his hair greying like old Papa's
And his hairline receding like an angry wave
Then he'll curse the poet who sang:
"I'll follow knowledge like a sinking star
Beyond the utmost bounds of human thought…"

For each grey hair,
He remembers a book
Buried in his memory
Like coins in the vault of a bank,
Or details in books of history—
These are times he would sing:
"I love my books I won't lie,
Inside them I'll live and die."

Lonely
Room at
Christmas

when nature calls,
she's afraid to obey—
for her, the lavatory is the
loneliest room in the planet.
inside, the walls are crowded
with invisible spiders spinning
webs that enmesh her in dreams.
afraid she shuts her eyes wishing
she could morph into a snail to hide
beneath the mollusc's protective shell.
instead, her heart becomes a braille she
reads with her fingers as mental eyes. scared, she
opens her eyes again to clear the fog in her head.
then she realises it's Christmas season and her Xmas
tree is waiting for mounting and decoration, in the corner.

November 11, 2006

Akwaaba*

You stand side by side,

Arms stretch out in supplication to ancestors,

Couple from the past, full of mysteries.

Akwaaba! Akwaaba! Akwaaba!

Poised like the crucifix, you

Welcome citizens and strangers,

Ancient dolls from Akan country,

Primordial icons of tradition and beauty,

We salute you...

We salute you,

Couple in communion with the living and the dead.

In the ridges of your matted hair, Mother Akwaaba,

Are paths to the past and to the future.

But where is your famed double axe motif—

Lost in a three-dimensional sculpture

Akin to your children lost in the wombs of the world

Swollen like your pouch of fertility?

Swollen like your pouch of fertility,

My mind ripens with thoughts of you in distant lands

---

* Akwaaba: See Noel Q. King's *Africa Cosmos: An Introduction to Religion in Africa.* California: Wadsworth Publishing Company, 1986, p.25. Akwaaba dolls originate from Akan region of Ghana and is venerated as national symbols.

Dreaming your invocation to unborn babies
To come suckle your firm breasts pointing
Like pins in grandma's sewing kit.
Akwaaba! Akwaaba! Akwaaba!
Husband and wife, twins of reincarnation,
United like the rings of skin on your necks.

Like the rings of skin on your necks
Your legends spiral beyond African shores
And your broad, circular faces chiselled by the artist
Echo the Chinese Ying Yang and their
Representations of celestial phenomenon—
Your aquiline noses smell the universe
Prompting your frowns against firearms and bloodletting
And united, you stand, side by side.

PART TWO:
Homeland Securities

Procession

The cycle begins
And memories return
With the procession—
Haunting
Hostile corridors
Of the cavernous
Dungeon that

me –
    and –
er

to Point of no Return.

The offspring of lucky survivors return
After centuries of

Forced
        Departures

And before a memorial altar
Erected by kinsmen
Recite names of heroes & heroines
Prior to laying wreaths
Of emancipation.

The pains persist
Tracing countless nights
Of brutalities –
The harsh chains choking and clanging
The slaves crying and grumbling...

Voices ricocheting on
Stonewalls of yesteryears' scars.

Long faces on eternal procession
Lost children reuniting
With the homeland,
Welcome!

My chest palpitates
Like the furious waves
Determined to erode the castle
And frothing with bloody histories of death

Look –
Here is where the slave ship anchored
And the blighted memory returns
Calcifying with the spirits of the castle —
The spirits departed
The spirits returned
Wizened by terrors of the middle passage
Shorn of the capes of fear
At Cape Coast.

Look again—
A dark priest
Offers garlands of leaves
Plucked
From the chest
Of the forest.

Listen–
You will hear
Distant voices
From distant pilgrims
Deracinated from Mother Africa
And planted in New Worlds
Where jewelled Capital plays God.

And the procession retreats...

Outside, the menacing canons are quiet
But in the mind
They explode with
Memories so-coloured with bile
They question Reconciliation
And call for Reparations

I cringe...
Trying to sort out piles
Of jagged images

Before humble guests
In a castle filled with ghosts
Of a horrible era

And where do I go from here
Wearing this necklace
Of lacerated memories

Where do I go
Bearing this cross
Of ancestors who crossed
Or perished without fearing
Death by water?

Where do I go?
In the horizon
Badagry beckons

Aided by tongue-tied
Fortes of lost souls.

I shall return to you, Cape Coast,
To listen to the sea and the wind
Forever telling tales of
Race. Greed. Cruelty.

Band of Worshippers

At Mama Bomboy's street corner shack,
They call every evening,
Proverbial wayfarers so heavily burdened
But with no one to give them rest.

First to call this evening is Awalu,
Tall, dark Fulani man with hazel eyes
Telling muted stories of a pilgrim,
Tenant of memories of miseries.

Next is Samanja, so named after his
Legendary walrus moustache curved
Upwards at the corners, pointing heavenwards
And accusing God of complicity in his painful fate.

And then there are half a dozen others—
Slaves of paraga, herbal alcoholic brew
Advertised by Mama Bomboy
As gbogboshe, a cure for all ailments.

Before every gulp they pour libations
In salutation to the guts
And for each gulp they hope for renewal
After a back-breaking day at the construction site.

Every shot is for the famished road
But "the last is for missus," a potent
Mix of gburantashi, an aphrodisiac,
Taken to make war, not love.

Then once upon a cold harmattan evening,
The band of paraga worshippers arrived at their haunt
And found the site razed by the General's bulldozers
Paving the ground for an officers' mess to sprout...

Independence Day 2006

It's October 1st again
And sad memories of aborted foetuses return
In an alien land he thinks of white-and-green colours
Of a nation in a season of scorch
Against the backdrop of approaching
Winter and its promise of pneumonia
Then he revisits the tale of the wanderer who left
His homeland with a promise of homecoming.

It was on the first market day
That he packed his thoughts and left
A pilgrim with old tunes playing in his heart.
Not that it was too late for breakthroughs
On the 46th season of old mistakes
But the petrifying news of another assassination,
And the breaking news of Reverend Ugo King's
'Spiritual immunization' of vulnerable
        miracle-seekers by whipping
Unhinge his mind already weary from
The stabs of unpaid wages and rising debts,
And loving Christ as the need arises.

It's October 1st yet again
And sad memoirs of a

Stillborn generation return,

In an alien land he thinks of paid minstrels

Strumming praise songs for General President

Dancing on the portals of Aso Rock

Drunk with euphoria of his inflated achievements.

It is the last market day

And in a foreign land

He gathers his roving thoughts

Filled with nostalgia —

He dreams dragon-ridden chambers of power

His heart a blaze of rainbows

For his tortured homeward journey.

New Yam Call
(For Uche Nduka)

Except by rooting how do you

Pluck yam tubers from their base?

—Christopher Okigbo

It was an ordinary phone call

Out of the whirlpool of Europe, yet his

Words were like invocations of Ifejioku,

Ancient god of rich yam harvest.

It was Anyanwu's voice, flower child

With songs of experience, exhorting

A straying son-of-the-soil to join in the festival,

To revive residues of an endangered tradition.

Ekwutosi's son, poet-prophet of Bremen,

I hear you chanting the book of Proverbs:

"Ants are creatures of little strength

Yet they store up their food in summer.

Locusts have no king

Yet they advance together in ranks.

The lizard can be caught with the hand

Yet it is found in kings' palaces."

But homeland overflows with black gold and eggheads,
Yet blindfolded *militicians* ungovern the land.

Uche, nwa Okija, when you break new yams in alien land
What do you tell the ancestors whose shrines are daily defiled?
What do you tell starving children who age in infancy,
And mothers whose pots are as dry as the Sahara?
What do you tell brides whose pride succumb like Domitila's,
And men whose manhood disappear through mystical handshakes?

Between a strutting hen and a
Bleating he-goat what's the difference?

O votary, we're converts holding bibles not Ikengas
When will you return to propitiate Ogwugwu Okija
Now desecrated by villainous politicians and false priests
Whom the gods promise elephantiasis of the scrotum?
When you speak of new yam festival in Bremen
Remember the shrine registers confiscated by the police—
Whose names are there, citizen of Anambra?
Do you know your state's now nest for measly hirelings
Who care less about Ifejioku and the ancient pantheon?

I hear your message, poet of irreverent verse.
Here in Edmonton I'm learning your new trinity—
Living, Loving, Mischief!
But loneliness has become my cold bed
Night after night I warm my life with poetry

Conjuring love in a season of nightmares
And how would I remember it's new yam season
When the aroma of burgers and muffins fill the air?

O Anyanwu, every day is a concert of desires
And your voice singing on the phone is a signifier
Out of the vortex of Europe, invoking Ifejioku,
And other ancient gods to prove their potency.

High Walls and Barb Wires

Festive December speeds by
And busy beaches tell no lies
Nor do they bare lovers' secrets;
Across the sands of Bar Beach
Victoria's secrets are hidden
Behind huge, barb-wired walls
And you can hear a vendor's
Compact disc player shouting
Across the walls in Victoria Island:
"I love my country I no go lie
Na inside am I go live and die…"

Those are ironic signs
Of homeland securities,
Citizens of fear and diasporas,
My homeland, my lover—
Tattooed as scars on my right arm
A crude gift six Decembers ago
From armed bandits
In search of Xmas gifts.

Between the beach and
The barb-wired walls
Xmas is an equation of sorts

Like US-Mexico border fence
The borderlines come and go.
Festivities may be in the air
But so are fears and nostalgia

Entwined with Soyinka's song:
"I love my country I no go lie
Na inside am I go live and die..."

In Evil Hour

(A prose poem)

The old pendulum clock swings toward the third hour after midnight—

The terror of their usual gate-crashing revisits—rag tag rogues emboldened by gruesome guns that sputter fire, bile and blood. It's New Year's Eve and the marauders are on parade again— warriors at night, cowards by day!

"Open the gate or we go melt am with Almighty acid," hollers Mopol, gang leader and Death's agent—a scarlet bandana on his head, an AK47 in his hand.

'They've come again in evil hour," Nneka, my wife, breaks out in tongues, in supplication to the God that answereth by fire.

And it begins to rain, a strange December rain, hissing as it kisses dust, soon droning like the wails of a mother who's lost her only son.

"They've come again, always at this evil hour—lost souls of apocalypse. May thunder consume them before day..." Nneka's voice fades with the rain, floating like garbage on a Lagos carnal.

Gba-ra-ra-ra! Gba-ra-ra-ra! Gba-ra-ra-ra! Raucous stammer of a gun shroud her echoing words as I remember the phone, dumb like a morgue, hiding in a corner...

In the horizon, sirens, ra-ta-ta-ta-ta and whistling and scampering...

In the cot, baby Bimbo babbles carefreely as if in conversation with receding thunder and the ra-ta-ta-ta-ta of police guns—Nneka kneels, this time, in thanksgiving to God, the Redeemer.

Stone Country

I do not know how
      to count bones
       on a heap of stones,
but I know how to howl
when I'm spirit-filled.

Lord, we've hollered
      for divine mediation,
       praying for a country
in distress, but this stress
would not pass away.

This is our country,
homeland dotted
      with activists' blood-stains
      and groaning from pains
caligraphed by low men in power.

This is our country,
and this internal occupation's
going to end soon—
the blood of martyrs will
bond their bones to stones.

Oil and Guns

(With flute and soft rattles)

There's greed enough to gnaw away the whole earth,

Soon no nature left.

—Nguyen Duy, "Metal, Wood, Earth, Water, Fire."

WOMAN:
You shall know them
by the oil stains on their guns
and the blood on their hands:
they are from the killing
fields of the Delta where
the sea oozes pollutants at dawn,
and the earth is a soggy loam
tired of neglect, unfit for building.

MAN:
You shall know them
by the denomination
of their foreign currency
and the oil-stained documents
in their golden briefcases:
they are expats and bunkerers,
political hirelings and cultists.

WOMAN:

You shall know them

by the badges of rape on

their shoulders, soldiers

from Odi and other

war zones in the Delta.

And what is oil without guns?

What is petrodollar without blood?

MAN:

I see them

from the sidelines—soldiers

and profiteers—

riders to hell hovering

like vultures waiting for carrion.

And what is oil without guns?

What is petrodollar without blood?

WOMAN:

Tonight, they are circling the sky again

looking for flashpoints of oil deposits.

Tonight, they are lost in their greed

waiting for relief by the river bend

and a chance to mend

their rigs and sing their credo

for new crude oil reserves.

MAN:

And what is oil without guns?

What is petrodollar without blood?

Where the Niger Weds the Benue

in Lokoja,

confluence town

where fishes sing at dusk

and two rivers wed,

you will not spot the famed

Niger

and

Benue

in that mysterious handshake

nor trace their interminable

embrace like two lovers

so distinct and yet so alike.

yet, there they are,

two rivers sharing

centuries of secrets,

synchronizing peacefully—

> there are some harmonies in Nature
>
> they just make you surrender in worship.

Homeland Securities

Security is mortals' chiefest enemy.
—William Shakespeare

today a grey weather camouflages time
and i track the uneasy mangrove swamps
from the Garden City where poisoned
flowers transfigure into bullets and blood
to Buguma, frightened by the frothing
waters as the speedboat churns its way and
the innocent water laughs with shy waves
oblivious of the fate that's befallen her.

i witness new pollutants thicken the sea
as a boil ripening, sack the fishermen
with their worn-out nets and perfume
the hooded creeks reeking of gunpowder
crystalline salt and suppliant hostages.
aerial roots of halophytic plants plead
for protection from the rippling, septic sea
as muse-ings over homeland securities
overwhelm me, lost in my mourning sickness.

it's dawn in the creeks and the fear of embittered
militants is the beginning of safety.
youths *immunized* against bullets by Egbesu,
faces laced with ancient magical symbols,

chant subversive litanies and contest the feds'
control of Nature's honeyed gifts to them.

tenants in their homeland, you will not dare
stare at the amulets tied around their necks,
nor question the potency of the warrior spirit—
here're the new faces of homeland securities, rag-tag
citizens of a country sewn with fabrics borrowed
from ethnic nationalities like a coat of many colours.

the boat cruises with my sailing thoughts as an odd
poem yearns to be written on the tablet of the mind.
i think of Odi where there are no road signs
but ruthless graffiti in charcoal, chalk or etched with
 some pin-point item by an insane army: "Weep not Odi,"
"The God almighty is the destroyer of any manmade god."
And laugh not or so do at your own peril: for you
will learn the meaning of homeland securities
under a leaking green-white-green
    umbrella
        in the gathering storm.

it's dawn in the creeks and news of another kidnap
floats through the cobwebbed airwaves as i track
the mangrove swamps from Garden City to Buguma.
"In the Niger Delta," says the newscaster,
"there's no security, only gangs, guns, and oil."

A Fever in the Blood

"You with your blend of chalk and rot,

You, bony scandalmonger, how can

You ever understand a fever in the blood?"

— Marina Tsevtayeva, "Ophelia: In Defence of the Queen"

Some day you'll meet her in the street—

She's the fever in my blood, semi-visible

Like the earring holes on your earlobes.

She bears her fate like an unwilling heroine.

You'll see her, lips taut from undecided laughter,

Sometimes happy, sometimes pensive,

A philosopher before her time, carrying

Life's burdens as a hawker without a buyer.

Some day you'll meet her to align with or malign.

Some day you'll meet her to align with or malign.

You'll see her at crossroads singing the rhyme:

> Row, row your boat

> Gently down the stream,

> Merrily, merrily, merrily, merrily,

> Life is but a dream.

A hesitant chorister, you will join the chorus

You whose heart is a mind grenade, a filthy

Closet filled with skeletons itching to stick out,
You'll un'stand how the fever runs in my blood.

You'll un'stand how the fever runs in my blood
When you see her through eyes blurred by guilt
You'll unsheathe not the blade that's your tongue
For she'll bake your dreams with childlike songs
Animate spaces in the cold oven that's your heart
She'll be the logic for forgiveness
Singer of hymns, fever in my blood,

Some day I'll be done with this act of contrition
Some day you'll meet her in streets of reunion.

Mind Grenades

I bite like a tick
you must tear out of
my roots to be rid of me
    —Marina Tsevtayeva, "Poem of the End"

Sardonic feelings zip through
as I sit, ruminating on a life that's
become a machine-gun of sorrows.

Daily I stride across streets of despair,
every stretch a battle line of landmines,
my mind threatening to detonate
from grenades of disillusionment.

I have lived this feeling,
a burnt-again adolescence.
Sad thoughts are the lice in
my unkempt mind, littered with
debris of fractured dreams.

"I'd rather be mad than enjoy myself," said
Antisthenes, Socratic commonsense realist.
I've become so familiar with the line
like a nostril used to snuff, have
haboured the idea since love left me

floundering on dreamscapes of pain.

If I do not write about laughter and joy,
forgive me, dear reader, for sorrow
is the tick biting this heart you must
tear out to be rid of it quickly.

Sailing

They were
two sunbirds
standing by the brook—
Jolly wore black like night
Jill glowed like yellow sky
A small paper boat
They would set to sail
like mountaineers in search of new life
but each time it somersaults
Jill would curse "the fickle, paper boat."

Jill would curse "the fickle, paper boat"
each time it somersaults
like mountaineers in search of new life
They would set to sail
A small paper boat
Jolly wore black like night
Jill glowed like yellow sky
Standing by the brook—
Two sunbirds
they were.

PART THREE:
Four Water Poems

I. Thinking of Iyi Oda*

Where is the road that leads to Iyi Oda,
village stream that watered my being,
where the water clings to your feet,
a child in need of loving-kindness.

I shall return to you, Iyi Oda, peaceful brook
where every morning was a conference
of boys and girls lost in their innocence
unmindful of their birthday suits.

I shall return to you, watermaid,
to read my book of life to your silent rhythm
unbroken by years of desertion.

I think of you in an alien land,
recalling every dive with mists
spreading like halos above my head.

I think of you, Iyi Oda...
How I wondered how you came
Through thickets smelling like damp armpits.

———————————

*   Stream in the poet's homeland, Ogwashi-Uku in Delta State, Nigeria.

Sometimes you played windsongs, whistling like a kettle
heaving with boiling water and sowing desire in my loins.
Then, I longed to drop into your watery bosom
and blossom from your fetishes of love.

Iyi Oda, wish you could stretch your warm arms to me here,
curl around me, lost in a shrinking and sinking planet in peril,
where each day the sun bakes a climate of fear
and lumberjacks shun the sweet scents of the forest.

Where is the road that leads to Iyi Oda,
where the fishes are shy, flashing like my eyelids
and swimming in a hide-and-seek style.

Village stream that watered my childhood,
I will return to you, penitent, for my final cleansing.

II. Teardrops

The cleansing begins with a teardrop -
Nature's watery pearls drop
Springing from his eyes before they pop
In salutation to grief.

She's been long gone
To where she belongs.
Watermaid with a heart of rock,
He'll write you into his bleeding book.

"When was the last time you cried?"
His little girl asked. "Daddy, you make me want to cry too."
Her eyes are a dripping tap
Each droplet landing like a full-stop.

There are no commas in grief
And tears know no punctuation
They are like July rains
That fall in Lagos at random.

"Misfortunes never come singly," he quotes,
His life a stammer of squashed hopes
In search of happiness he found the sea
And Mammywata, weird water woman.

And the cleansing begins with a teardrop

And riders to the sea know the value of water.

III. Meeting the Pacific at Point Reyes
(For Lee Swenson, tour guide and marvelous host)

Sitting by the Pacific at Point Reyes
the mind rummages its two-and-a-half miles depth
as the sea spreads its wide mysteries
through one-third of the earth's surface.

In the horizon, clouds and water in combat
invoke the fate of Ferdinand Magellan
on that day when filled with sea sickness,
the famed explorer blurted: "Mare Pacificum."

At Point Reyes, I see the sea is truly "peaceful;"
today, the water ripples as if caressed by a lazy wind,
and the grasses kissing the borders of the beach
Sway and hiss respectfully to Nature's songs.

Maryana, the Ukrainian, picks California blackberries
as Lee locates Point Reyes Lighthouse in the fog,
a 37-foot testimony to human challenge of nature.
Queyn, thinking of Vietnam, writes his
daughter's name on the beach sands.

And I, troubadour of many colours,
think of Lagos Bar Beach where every
holiday, Olookun takes a swimmer for sacrifice
and the Atlantic, ever hungry, eats our land.

But at Point Reyes, there are no
signs of the shrinking ocean; no
sounds of any plate tectonics below
only Nature in its aquatic splendour.

I will return to your watery Majesty, Pacific,
A wanderer in search of oceanic secrets,
and like Pablo Neruda, "I yearn only
to become the incarnation of marine stone."

IV. The Sea Bears Many Secrets
(For Nneka, who was murdered and dumped into the Atlantic)

No one knew when the butcher called,
hireling from a budding secret cult,

by day is human and friend,
but at night, a bloodthirsty fiend.

You listened, following fate like the wind,
sowing friendship and reaping no pity.

Then you walked into a hideous bind
where beasts reign over a garden city.

You didn't prepare for the mortal embrace
and so you departed your room with grace,

beauty, with a head loaded with knowledge
but not smart enough to know he wouldn't budge.

And so like John, you walked in evil hour
into the nest of a lovesick slaughterer

who with just one poisoned kiss of death
sucked your naive blood and sought

the sea to wash you down and wash him clean
knowing the sea bears many secrets like rain.

*   *   *

There are secrets buried in the vaults of seas -
treasures from sunken ships, treasures from
cities buried by cyclones and earthquakes

There are bones of drowned swimmers,
sailors, passengers and homicide victims...

There are amphibians, plants, plankton, skeletons, and minerals;
not even underwater archaeologists can hunt them all.

On their banks, too, are more secrets,
like the huge graveyard for five million victims
left on the Congo by Leopold II of Belgium.

You could have been one, Nneka,
disappearing without a farewell or a scar

but the sea is no resting-ground for you
and so the sea rejected you,
even with the stone strung on your waist.

You floated without a lifebuoy
to give testimony at nineteen,
just a term to graduation.

You floated like the seaweed,
seeking justice even in death
with nothing but a skewered heart.

The mourning time is not over yet
Every morning we think of you, and
Every water body recalls your sordid exit.

The sea may bear many secrets
But there are some it spits forth.

For Mama Kweke

"Earthly fame's like a smoke, I guess,"
Maria Akhmatova wrote, an epitaph
That haunts the world's eyes still. Though
The deadly hour came and she departed, no
One could bury both her body and her
Voice. She longed for immortality and
Earned it, and the smoke from her

Creative foundry continues to spiral.
Now she is your sister, Mama Kweke, so
On this page I plant a wreath for you
Beside her, where time and death unite
You, glad that in the Hereafter she'll teach
Your tender soul how to write poetry
And together you'll both tell the rosary—
She, with her Russian tongue, you

With your ancestral Igbo voice.
Mama Kweke, in death you earned enough
Epaulettes to make a general envious—you,
Strong woman with a generous heart,
Heroine of several battles. Your sonorous
Name still carries its song, invoking a
Funeral with a long procession of homage—
Payers. And I knew your transition had

Come with an unforeseen apotheosis. So I
Tell your offspring to weep not; but
Grief begins where crying stops and suspends
Belief in the resurrection. Tell me, Mama Kweke,
Does death know race, gender or class? In your
Conversations with Sister Maria do you have a
Translator? I will return to this question, Mama
Kweke, when the memorial hour comes. Adieu!

www.ingramcontent.com/pod-product-compliance
Lightning Source LLC
Chambersburg PA
CBHW020743160726
47993CB00006B/2593